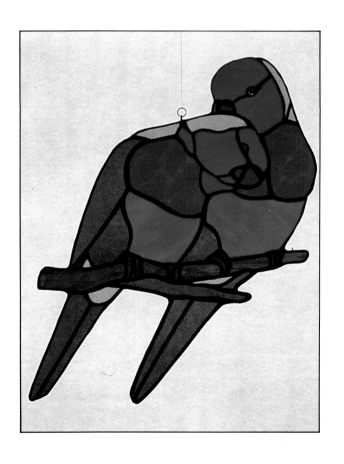

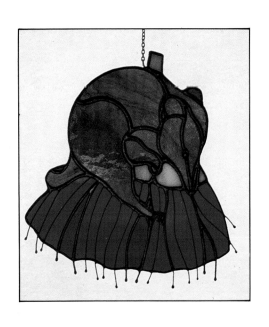

AUSTRALIAN BUSH BEAUTIES

JILLIAN SAWYER

**Designs for Stained Glass
Suncatchers**

**Published and Distributed by
FIREBIRD LEADLIGHTS**

(Printed in Western Australia)

Foreword

Thankyou for your support in making my first book, "Australian Leadlight Designs" such a success. Presented in this book, is an assortment of "Australian" suncatchers with common and scientific names included, some brief notes that may be of interest and a few helpful hints.

Fun to design, fun to make and ideal to give as gifts, suncatchers can be easy and quick to make, or as complicated and beautiful as you desire.

Remembering the old adage "practice makes perfect", suncatchers can be ideal practice pieces upon which to perfect your cutting and soldering techniques.

If you have only made panels and never a suncatcher, you will experience a freedom of design that will send your imagination soaring -- tails, ears, beaks can go virtually anywhere and how about those lovely pointed petals and leaves! With no background to worry about, your designs will impart a wonderful sense of realism. The sky's the limit -- hang them everywhere and let them "catch the sun".

Jillian Sawyer

For my daughter Kerin, with love.

Special thanks to Wayne for photography and to my husband Brian for his unfaltering support.

Distributors:
Firebird Leadlights
1030 Albany Highway
East Victoria Park WA 6101

Telephone: (09) 362 6259
Facsimile: (09) 362 6259

KOALA
(Phascolarctos cinereus)

This harmless and lovable
marsupial ranges from the tropics
to the cool, temperate regions of eastern Australia.
Hunted for their pelts, they were almost wiped
out until re-established by nature lovers. Ongoing
research will help to ensure this endearing species will continue to survive.

RAINBOW LORIKEETS
(Trichoglossus haemotodus)

Their rich brilliant colour and cheeky friendly ways have made this parrot a firm favourite. Commonly seen in suburban gardens in northern and eastern Australia, flocks are starting to build up in southern and western Australia as a result of birds escaping from private aviaries.

Head and lower front: Blue-purple
Breast: Red to streaky red-
　　　　　　　orange-yellow
Band: At back of head yellow-lime
Back: Bright green
Wings: Bright green
Beak: Red
Claws: Grey.

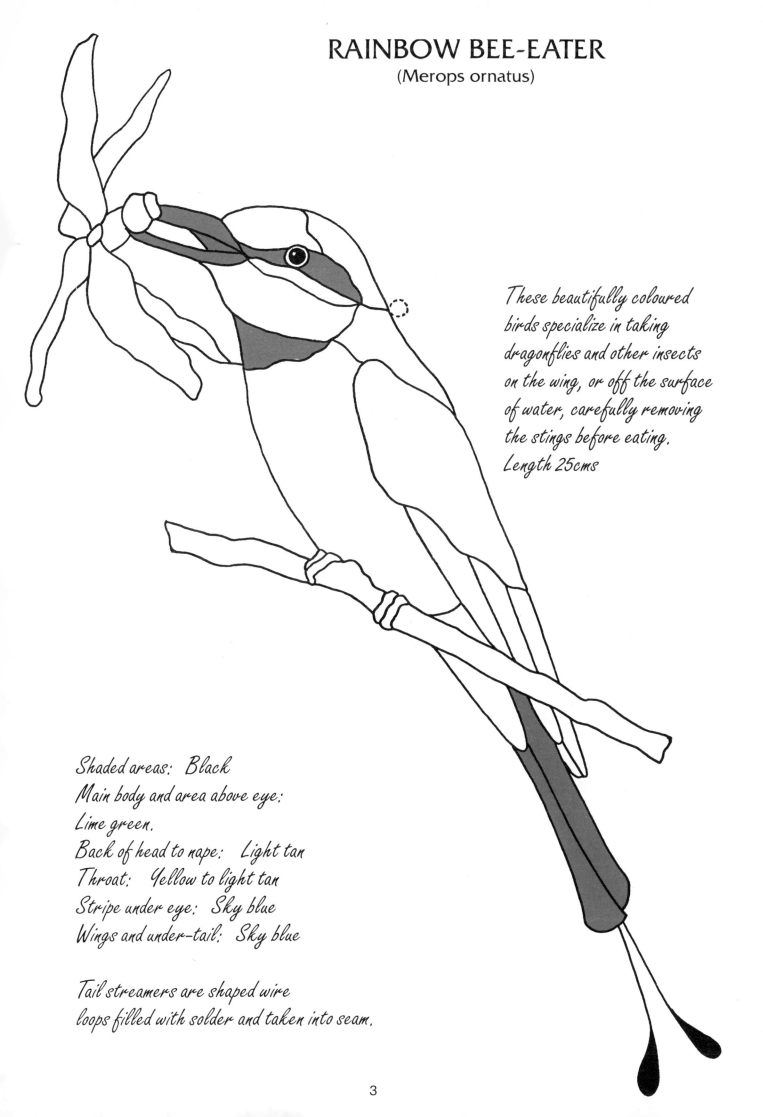

RAINBOW BEE-EATER
(Merops ornatus)

These beautifully coloured
birds specialize in taking
dragonflies and other insects
on the wing, or off the surface
of water, carefully removing
the stings before eating.
Length 25cms

Shaded areas: Black
Main body and area above eye:
Lime green.
Back of head to nape: Light tan
Throat: Yellow to light tan
Stripe under eye: Sky blue
Wings and under-tail: Sky blue

Tail streamers are shaped wire
loops filled with solder and taken into seam.

HONEY-POSSUM
(Tarsipes rostratus)

This tiny possum has no close relatives and appears to be the sole survivor of an extinct group of marsupials. It lives only in the south-west of Western Australia and has a long tubular snout and brush tipped tongue to enable it to probe the blossoms of the Eucalyptus in search of nectar.
Length 6-8 cms.

Tip of nose and claws solder filled and built up.
Stamens are tinned wire with solder blobs overlayed and attached last.

COOKTOWN ORCHID
(Dendrobium bigibbum)

Equally happy growing on trees or rocks in north-eastern Queensland and is the floral emblem for that state.

Shaded Areas Open

Re-inforce buds and stems with wire.

Flowers are pink to mauve with rare specimens being white.

BARN OWL
(Tyto alba)

Small mammals, insects, mice and birds are targeted by the Barn owl's silent flight.

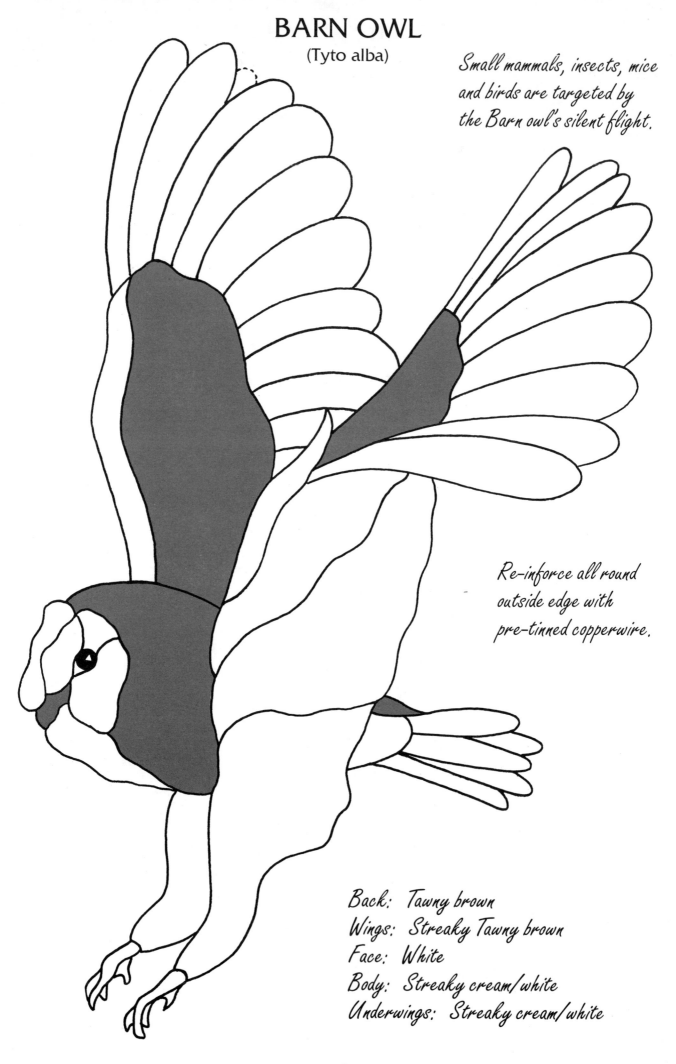

Re-inforce all round outside edge with pre-tinned copperwire.

Back: Tawny brown
Wings: Streaky Tawny brown
Face: White
Body: Streaky cream/white
Underwings: Streaky cream/white

BLACK SWAN (Cygnus atratus)

Inhabits eastern and western parts of continent, only venturing into central regions when rain fills inland lakes. Nest is a huge floating heap of vegetation, usually on lakes and swamps.

Glossy black
Beak: Red with white band
Wing tips: White
Cygnets: Fluffy grey

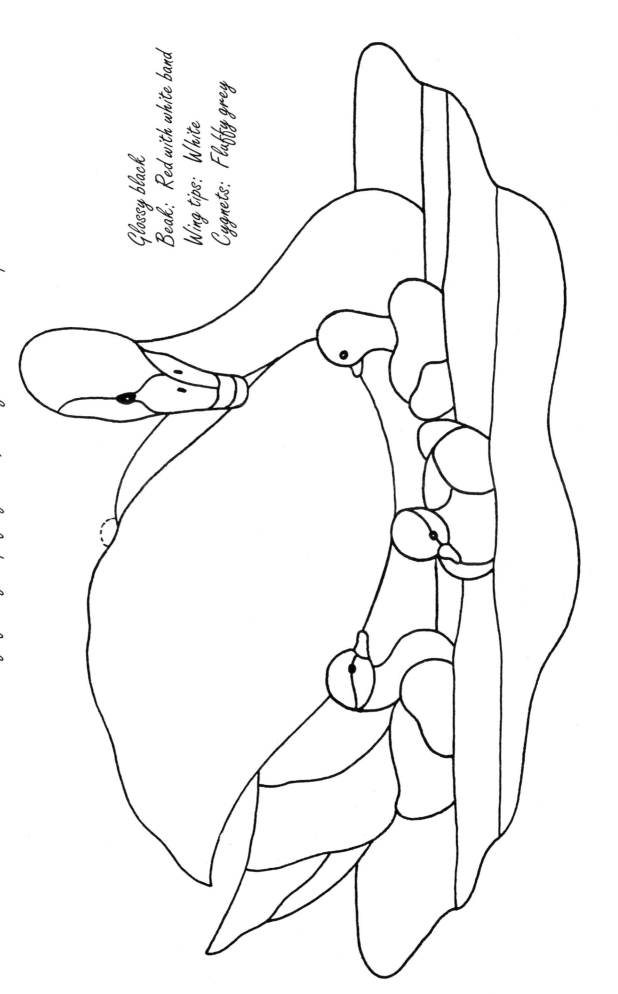

7

ULYSSES BUTTERFLY
(Papilio ulysses)

One of the largest
of Australia's
butterflies and favours
the outskirts of rainforests.

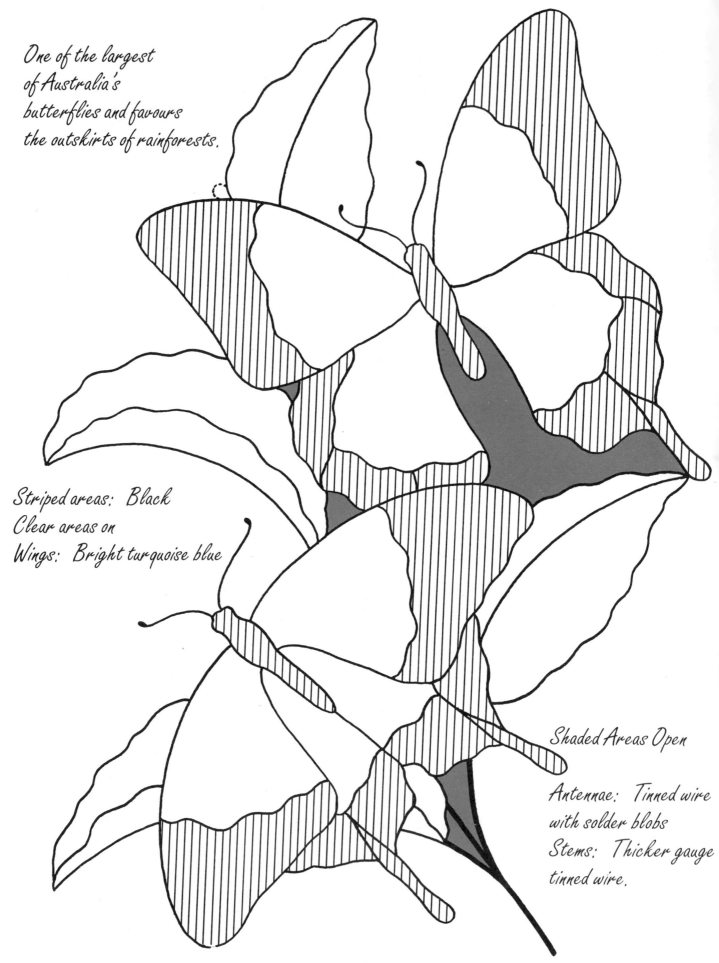

Striped areas: Black
Clear areas on
Wings: Bright turquoise blue

Shaded Areas Open

Antennae: Tinned wire
with solder blobs
Stems: Thicker gauge
tinned wire.

8

KANGAROOS

There are approx. 48 species of kangaroos, wallabies and their relatives, collectively known as macropods (big feet), Australia wide.

Few sights equal the grandeur of a mob of roo's thundering over a sea of yellow grass or a desert of red sand.

PARAKEELYA and COPPERCUPS
(Calandrinia species)   (Pileanthus peduncularis)

Habitat:

Sandy soils in arid areas

Parakeelya the larger flower
here. Bright cyclamen
pink with yellow centre.

Coppercups the smaller flowers
and buds here. Coppery burnt
orange with darker centre.

This bouquet can be hung
from almost any seam
with equal effect.

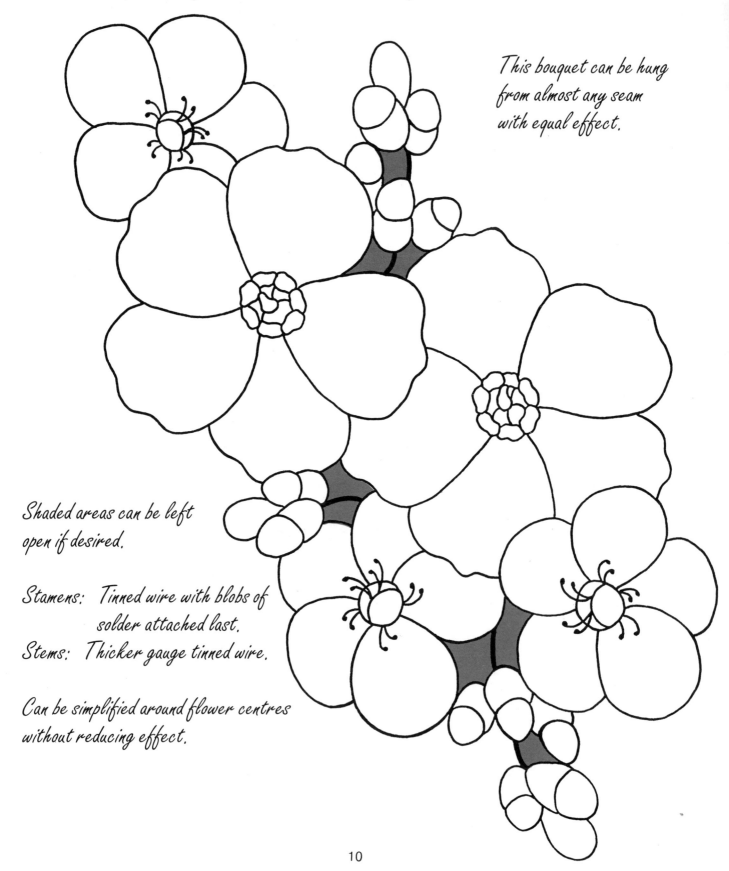

Shaded areas can be left
open if desired.

Stamens: Tinned wire with blobs of
solder attached last.
Stems: Thicker gauge tinned wire.

Can be simplified around flower centres
without reducing effect.

LACE MONITOR

(Varanus varius)

Sunning on log

Also called the TREE CLIMBING GOANNA

"Goanna" is a name peculiar to Australia and thought to be a corruption of the Spanish "Iguana", meaning "Lizard".

At 2 mtrs long, the lace monitor is the second largest goanna after the Perentie and spends much of its time climbing trees looking for bird's nests.

Habitat: Forests and coastal tablelands of eastern Australia.

Blue–black bands alternating with cream, yellow or orange areas.

COMMON WOMBAT (Vombatus ursinus)

in tree-root burrow

Supposedly shares ancient common ancestor with the Koala, which took to the trees, whilst the wombat chose a life of burrowing and feeding on ground plants.   Length 900mm.

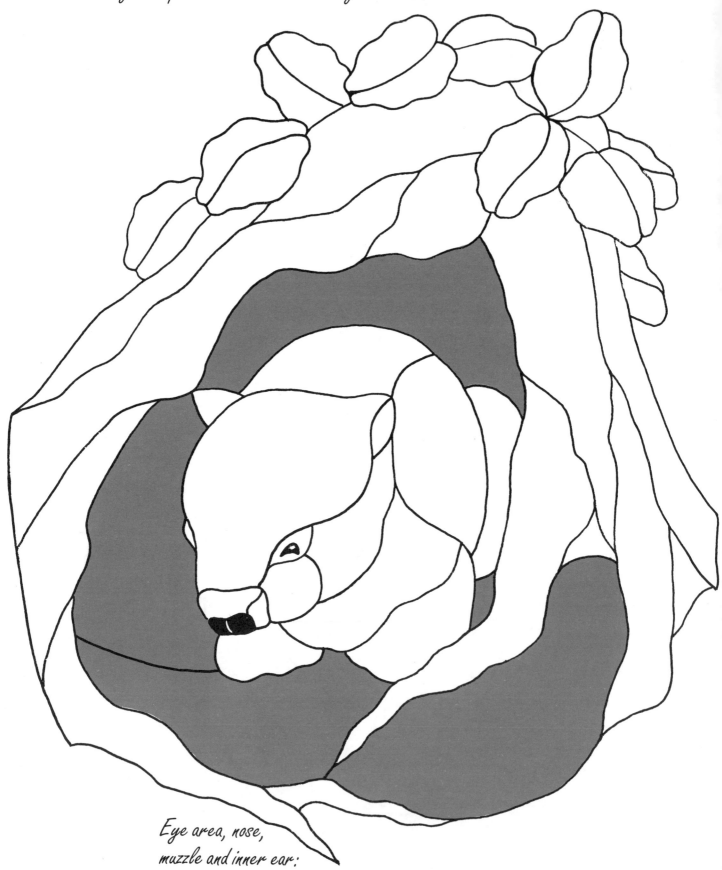

Eye area, nose, muzzle and inner ear: Pinkish skin coloured, with eye being painted.

AZURE KINGFISHER
(Ceyx azureus)

One of only two Australian Kingfishers who are exclusively hunters of aquatic prey, the Azure Kingfisher gathers food from the rivers, creeks and estuaries of the wetlands.

With Australia being so arid, Kingfishers have been able to inhabit the rest of the continent only by developing dry land hunting habits.

KANGAROO APPLE

(Solanum aviculare)

Habitat: Wet forests and rainforest margins in Queensland, New South Wales and Victoria.

Shaded Areas Open.

Can be hung from almost any seam with equal effect.

Always take hanging loop into solder seam for extra strength.

14

SPLENDID WREN
(Malurus splendens)

Also known as Black-backed or Splendid fairy wren.
The male is the most spectacular of all of the Australian fairy
wrens but the female is dull brown.
Needs tracts of low, shrubby vegetation for survival.

Length 12cm.

Due to fineness of twigs, leaves etc., it is strongly recommended
that these areas and indeed the whole piece be reinforced with wire,
if made as a suncatcher.

Thin stems from leaves are tinned
copper wire.

LONG-TAILED PYGMY POSSUM
(Cercartetus caudatus)

On branch of Black Bean Tree
(Castanospermum australe)

Quite numerous, but seen infrequently, this attractive little creature occurs in north-eastern Queensland. Length including tail 23cms.
Body: Reddish brown to grey, dark around eyes.
Nose and Paws: Pink.
Blossoms: Pinkish-orange, yellow base and buds.

Shaded areas left open.

16

ELECTUS PARROTS
(Electus roratus)

Male and female plumage so different,
that for a long time these birds
were thought to be separate species.
Only found in north eastern
Australia, but common in limited rainforest areas.

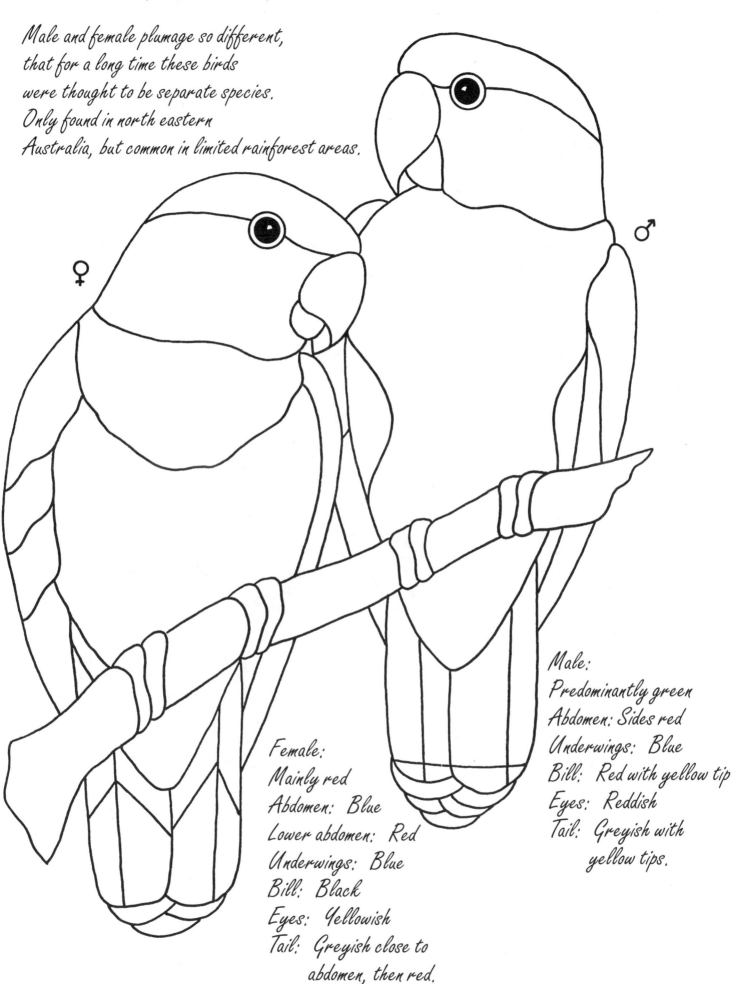

Female:
Mainly red
Abdomen: Blue
Lower abdomen: Red
Underwings: Blue
Bill: Black
Eyes: Yellowish
Tail: Greyish close to
    abdomen, then red.

Male:
Predominantly green
Abdomen: Sides red
Underwings: Blue
Bill: Red with yellow tip
Eyes: Reddish
Tail: Greyish with
    yellow tips.

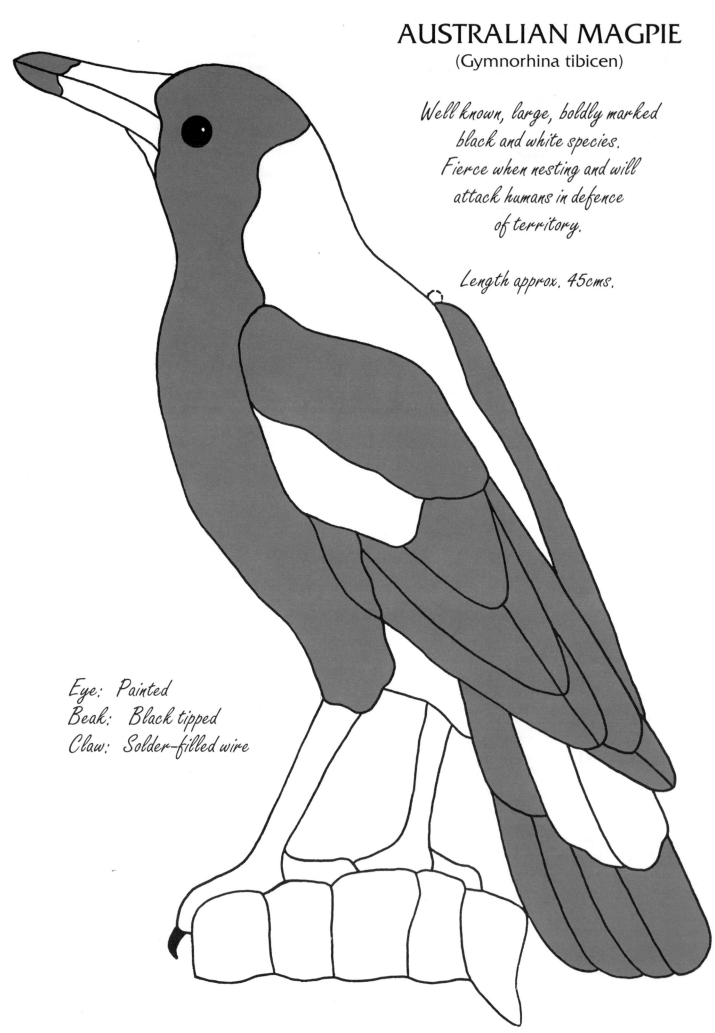

AUSTRALIAN MAGPIE
(Gymnorhina tibicen)

Well known, large, boldly marked
black and white species.
Fierce when nesting and will
attack humans in defence
of territory.

Length approx. 45cms.

Eye: Painted
Beak: Black tipped
Claw: Solder-filled wire

RED-EYED TREE FROG
(Litoria chloris)

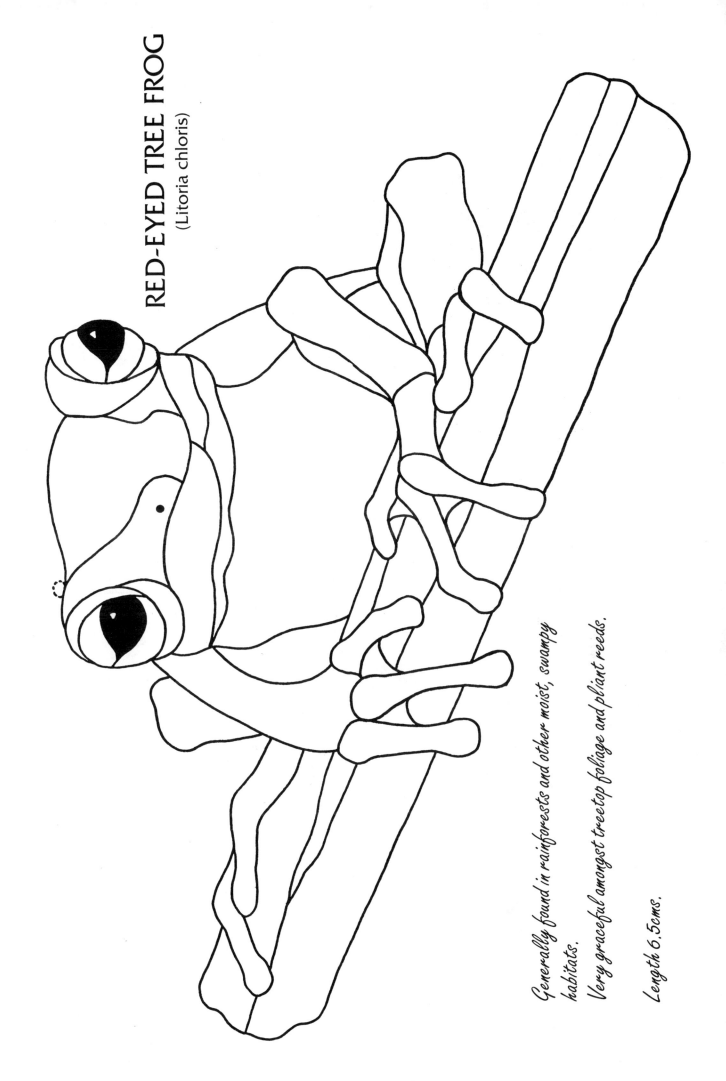

Generally found in rainforests and other moist, swampy habitats.

Very graceful amongst treetop foliage and pliant reeds.

Length 6.5cms.

AUSTRALIAN BIRDWING (Ornithoptera Priamus)

The largest Australian butterfly, the Birdwing is also one of the largest in the world. (The female's wings may span 200mm.) Birdwings normally inhabit rainforests and are butterflies of the air, flying high around the tops of rainforest trees.

Shaded areas: Black.

Striped areas: Golden orange yellow

Open areas: Bright green with lime tinge.

Antennae: Tinned wire with solder blobs

NATIVE ROSELLA
(Hibiscus heterophyllus)

Habitat: Rainforest margins, tall forests and riverbanks of the coast and tablelands of the east coast of Australia

Shaded Areas Open

Stamens: Tinned wire with solder blobs.

GALAH
(Eolophus roseicapilla)

Flocks of these much loved birds are a sight to behold as they bank and wheel in pink and grey clouds.

FRILLED-NECK LIZARD
(Chlamydosaurus kingii)

Spectacular display when threatened, with its impressive frill,
violent hissing and wide open mouth. When running on hind legs,
can move extremely quickly.
Habitat: Wooded areas in northern Australia, much time spent in trees.
Average length 70cms.

Grey or brown with lighter frill
(Eastern species) to reddish brown with yellow and orange
frill (Desert varieties). Bright yellow mouth lining.

SULPHUR-CRESTED
COCKATOO
(Cacatua galerita)

with Acorn Banksia
(Banksia prionotes)

*Common and familiar in northern
and eastern Australia with raucous
screech advertising presence and
sounding a noisy alarm if
disturbed.*

Length 50cms.

NUMBAT
(Myrmecobius fasciatus)

Under threat of extinction, this pretty, carnivorous marsupial, with a tail like a bottle brush and an appetite for termites, is now found only in a small area of south-western Australia.

Body: Reddish brown, with white bands separated by dark brown on back.
Face: Reddish brown, with dark stripe running through eye area. Striped above and below eye with white.
Tail and Hindquarters merging to darker brown.

Shaded areas left open.
Stems of tinned copper wire.

HEART-LEAF FLAME PEA
(Chorizema ilicifolium)

Found in sandy and gravelly
sites in forests of
south western W.A.

Top petals orange with
yellow eyes.
Bottom petals bright
cyclamen pink.

Shaded Areas Open

Buds are wrapped in tinned
wire for strength and soldered
into seam in leaf.

GREEN ROSELLA
(Platycercus caledonicus)

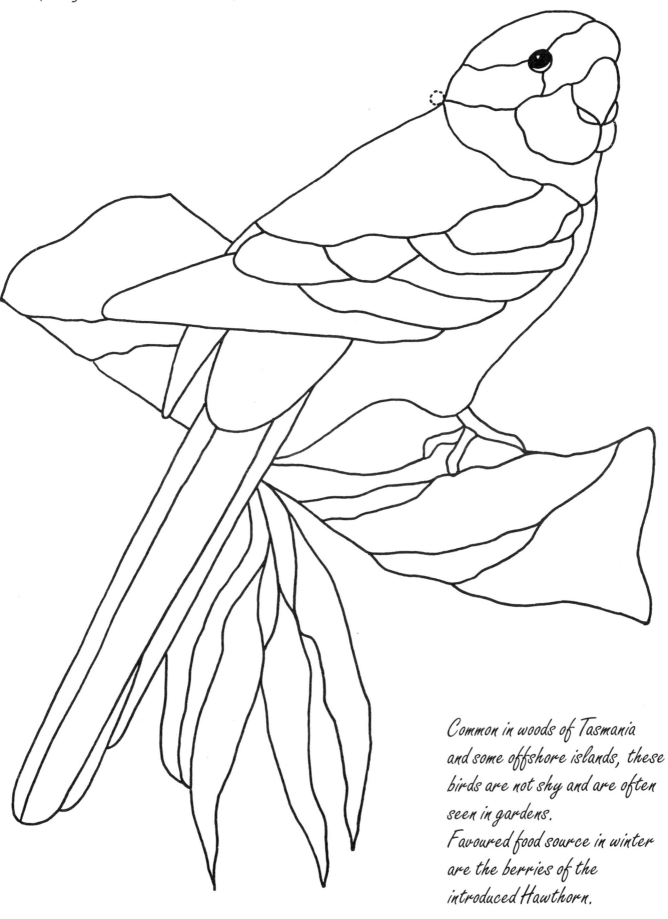

Common in woods of Tasmania
and some offshore islands, these
birds are not shy and are often
seen in gardens.
Favoured food source in winter
are the berries of the
introduced Hawthorn.

FUCHSIA GUM
(Eucalpytus forrestiana)

The arrangement of the brilliant red caps explains its common name.

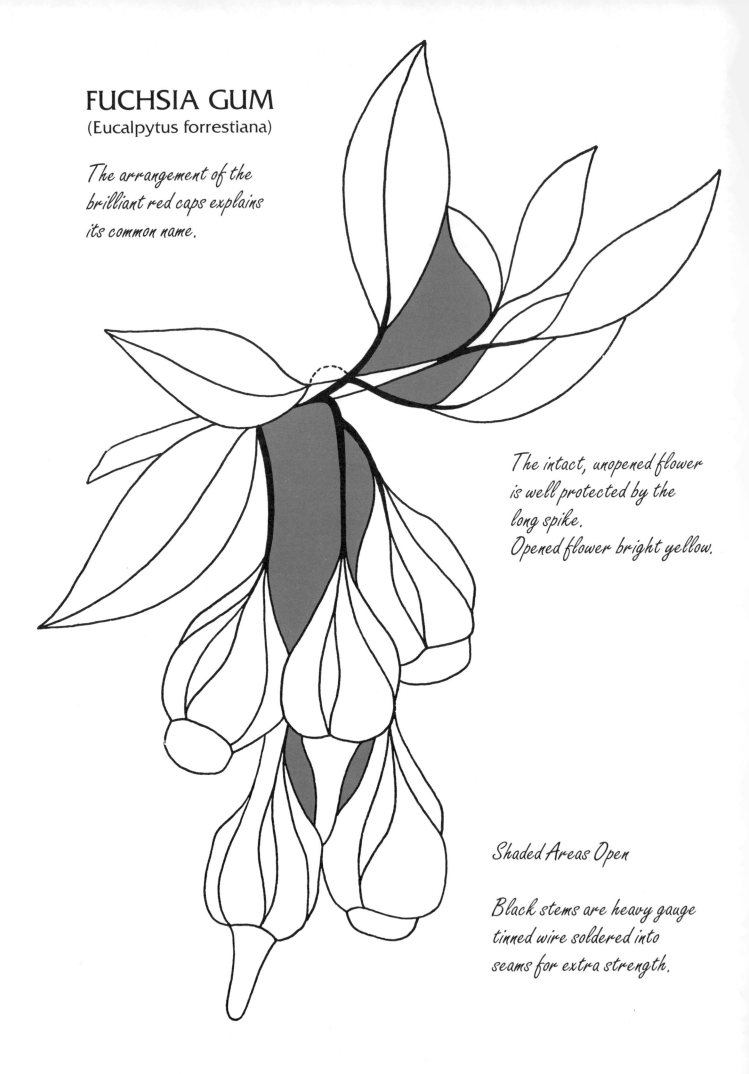

The intact, unopened flower is well protected by the long spike.
Opened flower bright yellow.

Shaded Areas Open

Black stems are heavy gauge tinned wire soldered into seams for extra strength.

RED-CAPPED PARROT
(Purpureicephalus spurius)

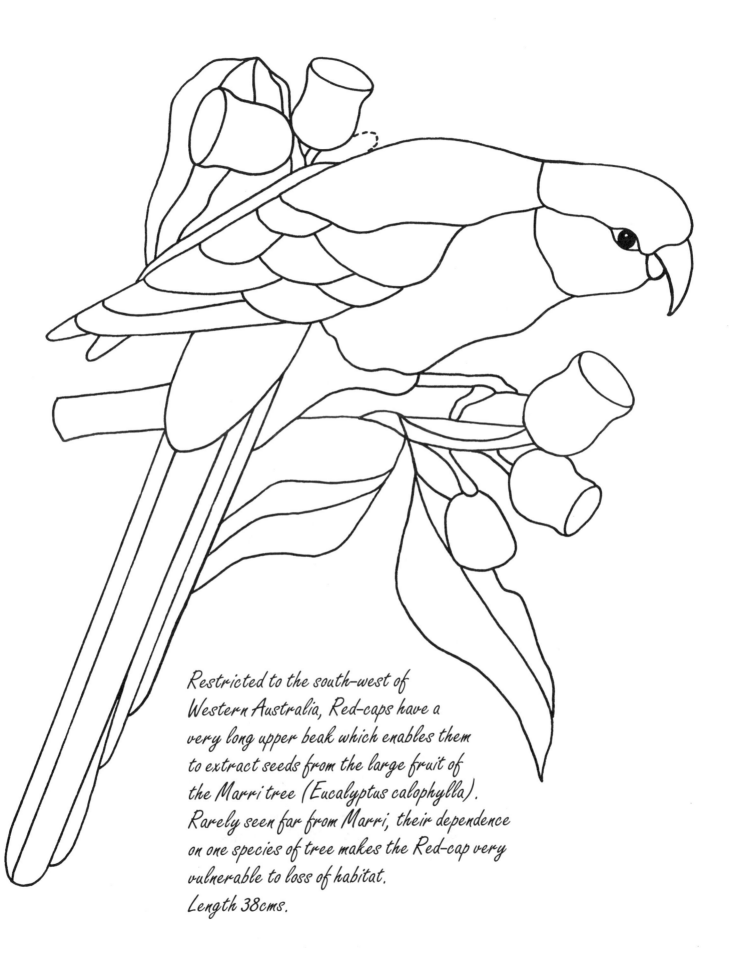

Restricted to the south-west of
Western Australia, Red-caps have a
very long upper beak which enables them
to extract seeds from the large fruit of
the Marri tree (Eucalyptus calophylla).
Rarely seen far from Marri, their dependence
on one species of tree makes the Red-cap very
vulnerable to loss of habitat.
Length 38cms.

GIANT or BLUE WATERLILY
(Nymphaea gigantea)

Habitat: East coast from northern Queensland to northern New South Wales in still water in rivers and ponds.

Flowers can be blue to mauve, pink or white. Centres: Yellow